What Others are Saying About
September Eleventh

"These striking and tender poems draw you back to the day no matter where you were. They exemplify why the poetry of witness, especially eyewitness, is always necessary. It's as though we all were back there twenty years ago, but here too, proximate across time, with Flynn as a wise guide, trying to help us see and think again about how it happened."
— Pamela Hart, author of *Mothers Over Nangarhar*
and writer-in-residence at the Katonah Museum of Art

❖　❖　❖

"Amalie Flynn's spare, clean words invite readers to share in her deeply felt experiences: fraught, urgent, and ultimately filled with optimism. Powerful and important reading for anyone hoping to better understand the contours of life in the 21st century."
— Adrian Bonenberger,
author of *The Disappointed Soldier and Other Stories from War*,
and a founding co-editor of *The Wrath-Bearing Tree*

❖　❖　❖

"With each poem, Amalie Flynn is 'making [her] memory chain' ... Throughout *September Eleventh*, the reader becomes witness to Flynn's struggles in finding answers to the unanswerable, witness to stories told while still grieving in the moment and twenty years later. We are beside her in each moment's struggle, connected by the chain."
— Lisa Stice, author of *Forces*,
Permanent Change of Station, and *Uniform*

Other Books You Might Like

Wife and War: A Memoir
by Amalie Flynn

❖ ❖ ❖

Hugging This Rock:
Poems of Earth & Sky, Love & War
by Eric Chandler

Permanent Change of Station
and *Forces: Poems*
by Lisa Stice

Our Best War Stories:
Prize-winning Poetry & Prose
from the Col. Darron L. Wright Memorial Awards
Edited by Christopher Lyke

SEPTEMBER ELEVENTH

an epic poem, in fragments
by
Amalie Flynn

Middle West Press LLC
Johnston, Iowa

❖   ❖   ❖

Poetry / Remembrance / Family & War

September Eleventh: an epic poem, in fragments
by Amalie Flynn
ISBN (print): 978-1-953665-06-5
ISBN (e-book): 978-1-953665-07-2
Library of Congress Control Number: 2021950789

❖   ❖   ❖

Middle West Press LLC
P.O. Box 1153
Johnston, Iowa 50131-9420
www.middlewestpress.com

❖   ❖   ❖

Special thanks to James Burns of Aurora, Colorado!
Your patronage helps publish great military-themed writing!
www.aimingcircle.com

For all who were lost,
lost on that day ...

and after

CONTENTS

Foreword

In journalism school, anniversary stories about significant past news events are sometimes decried as lazy assignments—indications of an unimaginative editorial mindset. You can, after all, practically set your clock by them. Decade after decade.

There is no denying, however, that anniversaries provide necessary cultural milestones—rare moments in which our fractious and distracted society can be compelled toward moments of collective mindfulness and remembrance.

Recognizing this reality, my former J-professors would provoke classroom discussions: If anniversary stories are a necessary evil, how can we make them less rote? Less predictable? More engaging? More helpful?

Expanding our scope, to include literature and art: How do storytellers keep individual and cultural memories alive, without sensationalizing trauma? How do we avoid relitigating political debates and over-reactions, to instead reflect on what a past event means—has come to mean—in the present? How do we avoid reopening wounds, to focus on healing?

As a fellow poet and war writer, I have long followed Amalie Flynn's artistic explorations of news and meaning. As a fellow editor of literary publications, I appreciate her curation of poetry at the monthly on-line journal *The Wrath-Bearing Tree* (wrath-bearingtree.com). There, she often pairs contributors' words with abstract visuals of her own creation. More than once, my own poems have benefited from her careful attentions there.

Still, I'm not sure I was fully prepared for the impact of Flynn's September 2021 multi-media experiment in on-line poetry, in which she revisited her first-person experiences of Sept. 11, 2001. For days and weeks after, in my social media feeds, Flynn's micro-videos would appear like prayer-flags or psalms. Each seemed to offer an opportunity for reflection, or even epiphany. Sometimes, I would experience a connection of empathy with the narrator. Sometimes, I would experience an association with my own memories.

Leave it to a poet to unlock something fresh and new in the space of "remember that day" stories—here is a narrative that both invites participants to recall their own experiences of a trauma in our nation's shared history, while also recreating the immediacies and uncertainties of what it was like to live through it.

In reformatting Flynn's project to printed pages and to e-reader screens, we looked for ways to replicate some of that magic.

Readers need not consume or digest Flynn's project all at once, nor even sequentially. Instead, they can choose to flip through pages almost randomly, in a fashion similar to how some might use the *I Ching* or Christian Bible. Certainly—for me at least—that method helps recreate the scatteredness of that day, as well as something of the essence of encountering Flynn's art on-line for the first time.

Each micro-poem is presented here in numerical order, each to its own page. On each page, readers of the e-book edition will also find an active URL website address linked to a companion micro-video posted on YouTube. Each video features presentations of text and audio voiced by Flynn herself.

Rather than input links manually—an admittedly clunky solution— readers of the print edition can access all the videos by scanning a QR code provided on pages xiii and 136.

— *Randy Brown, Editor*
December 2021

Artist's Statement

In 2001, I stood on a corner and watched 9/11 happen. I watched a plane hit. I watched the people jump. I watched the Towers fall.

In 2010, I began a year-long blog project called "September Eleventh" (septembereleventh.wordpress.com). Every day—for a year—I posted a micro-poem recounting my experience of witness.

In 2021, I returned to these micro-poems in commemoration of the 20-year anniversary, recreating and recrafting them into a series of 130 micro-videos—fragments that could be excavated, sifted through, and shared via e-mail and social media.

The words and my voice piece the event together like bones. Like body parts in the rubble. This print collection is an echo of witness. It is the poetry that comes after. It is the aftermath.

These poems are about what happened on 9/11 and what I saw and who I am now—who we all are—because of it.

—Amalie Flynn,
September 2021

"an epic poem, in fragments"

Find all of the companion videos
to these micro-poems on
Amalie Flynn's YouTube channel:

https://www.youtube.com/channel/
UCKNqU0BTVFLUNC6fA72pEXw/videos

1 –

I was there on 9/11.
On 9/11 I was there.
Not in the Towers
Not directly beneath
But close.
Proximity is a measurement of closeness
Of what is proximal – this point of attachment
The end of a bone.

https://youtu.be/KWtcdIbzRjw

2 –

I am standing on the corner of Church and Worth
Where the first street shoots out of the second street
Like a forearm out of a socket, like a bone from a socket.
Even from where I stand today
Even 20 years later
20 years after 9/11
It is close.

https://youtu.be/oICYB-AggpY

3 –

I am still too close just like I was then
On that day
I am still too close to it.
To the impact to the dust to all of it.
What was unsettled then remains now
In my lungs and in my memories close.

https://youtu.be/wwCfbkP1ehU

4 –

I am a writer.
I write stories.
The Twin Towers were 110 stories tall.
They had 110 stories each.
That is this
220 stories together.

https://youtu.be/98b3hq3Kh2Q

5 –

How do I count this?
Units or decimals or numbers
This is how we can count loss.
Reduce a body to this value.
Convert a body – use this system.
Counting loss like that ends up in this.
A fraction of what it was or should be.

https://youtu.be/TRsKZMA36B4

6 –

And ask. Always ask
Ask how many. How many
People and lives and stories were
In those two Towers, were in there?
There were too many people. There
Were too many stories to get down
Alive. They could not get out alive.
Now there are too many stories dead.

https://youtu.be/T-Zxz0L-YoQ

7 –

I cannot revise. When it is done
A story is done. Then it is time
To write a new story. Or this
The same story over and over.

https://youtu.be/w6MaseiEAPk

8 –

And now.
Now,
We cannot revise this.
We cannot quantify it
Or add it up in a way
That will make sense
Or make a meaning.

https://youtu.be/BVmSmEwWAwE

9 –

I can only tell it.
I can only tell you.
I want to tell you.
I have to
Tell you what happened.
Because it happened.
It happened.
On September Eleventh it happened.

https://youtu.be/OzNzpEGDDUU

10 –

New York City is a city.
It is the city it is your city
It is my city.
New York City is not a city.
It is a constellation of bodies on asphalt
In an unfolding sky of skin.
Displacement is where movement goes.
It is where you land where you end up.
This is where I always wanted to land.

https://youtu.be/kjP3Jz6YNEY

11 –

This is it.
That was what I was thinking
On that day on that morning looking up
To the sky when it happened.

https://youtu.be/Mkb2FnOu7xc

12 –

I miss New York City
Like the atmosphere created in a bed with sheets
And twisting and blankets that wrap around me
Like they wrap around her, the lady in the water.
New York City is where I became myself more
This statue of my own liberty.
Like it wraps around me still
Still that city still that sky.

https://youtu.be/EG1PYeMoReI

13 –

How can I fall away? How
Can I fall away from this?
Away from there and this?
Memories of planes sliding
Slowly crossing the sky or
People falling falling down
And sliding down the sides
Of those two giant Towers
Falling down the steel sides.

https://youtu.be/CJmJN954Qf8

14 –

Every thing gains speed eventually.
Even bodies controlled by the force
Of gravity that is greater than desire
Or the design of a dream.
And then.
And then they were gone.

https://youtu.be/AGZ1CK-cHro

15 –

How can I fall past this?
Past those two Towers on fire
Past the collapsing blue sky
Past New York City, my exploding diorama
Of bodies and of steel and that. That blue sky.

https://youtu.be/ve5oJw1Fqfg

16 –

New York City is a populous city.
It will always populate my heart
With its grid a geometry of possibility
Where everything can happen to you.
Everything. Even that.

https://youtu.be/D-Zce1gzGN4

17 –

The answer is this.
The answer is always this.
My answer is that
That I will never get away
That I will always be here
In my memories in that sky
In that bright blue morning
On September Eleventh.

https://youtu.be/t_usbGShymE

18 –

It was early and it was bright.
This was New York City in the morning
On that morning that it happened.

https://youtu.be/0P4pXmcfFzg

19 –

My apartment was on 79th Street
Next to the river where police boats will go
After this happens.
I walked that morning
To the subway just like,
Like every morning.

https://youtu.be/ukPxlpOqWN4

20 –

I walked down 79th Street
I crossed over York over
1st over 2nd and over 3rd until Lexington.
I walked two blocks south on Lexington
To the 77th Street station.
And then I went down
Down into the subway station
Down into darkness
And down into this
The beginning of a day this day.
The beginning of a memory this memory.

https://youtu.be/O1btEtCd2RE

21 –

I descended into the darkness of the station
And I am descending now
Again. I am there
Again.
I am here again. Standing on this platform
Floating in the sea of what happened.

https://youtu.be/nXg49g2LOHA

22 –

I remember boarding the 6 train
And taking it down to 51st
Where I switched to the E train
To take me down.
Take me down all the way.

https://youtu.be/cbh23BkVku8

23 –

I remember being on the train that morning.
I remember all of the bodies pressing against
Glass and metal and me.
I remember feeling it.
I remember the feeling of the cool seat against my thighs
And I remember all of the bodies and breath and stories alive.
I remember being alive.

https://youtu.be/0gb1f9rQ6tk

24 –

Memories are beads on a string.
I can tell you about my memories
Like beads.
About my grandmother in a flowered dress
Lying on a flowered couch before she died
And my other grandmother in a flowered
Folded lawn chair in her driveway before,
Before she died.
About a school bus and a girl decapitated
Almost
On the school bus in front of me
And about revival and how it fails.
About a truck dropping cow parts on a road
Slaughtered cows
Skinned limbs and heads rolling.

https://youtu.be/Fheso5mw_1U

25 –

Even this.
This is a string of my memories.
Beads like body parts rolling
Forming a chain that is going
That is still going on and interrupted
By planes and sky and what fell.

https://youtu.be/E65HD3uY8qg

26 –

I am making a memory chain here.
Making memories march together
In some way that matters
So that it matters.

https://youtu.be/tIhSpmR8wq8

27 –

Here in this vault of space
Or lack of space disjointed
But entombed by you and by me
My memories are embalmed fixed.

https://youtu.be/YRlQvBHyuEE

28 –

I am doing this for you.
I am doing this for me.
I am doing this for them.
I am doing this because
My memories are
My memorial.

https://youtu.be/AEZyaepw6bk

29 –

The sky in New York City
Is different.
You do not always see it
The sky in New York City.
And that is why
That is why it is different
From other places
From other skies.

https://youtu.be/0ZuEUCjpr8I

30 –

When you do
When you do see the sky in New York City
It is not flat.
It is not a flat prairie of sky that stretches
Out endlessly.

https://youtu.be/-nOFWJ4Gysg

31 –

The sky in New York City is geometric.
It is sudden shapes of blue popping
Popping out from behind the silver
Skyscrapers and popping in between.

https://youtu.be/_6LhPKX98VY

32 –

The sky in New York City is shapes.
Buildings come up against each other
Creating the full blue empty in-between.

https://youtu.be/6bbqiY8N-xs

33 –

The New York City sky is this.
It is hexagons of blue falling.
It is the foreground
But it is the background
It is the positive and it is
The negative.
Add in the light,
That light.

https://youtu.be/UzDdxcsvZTw

34 –

Because sometimes light can take away
Stretching across a sky like gauze.
But this time the light reflected
Bounced off the silver skyscrapers
And filled the sky with more,
More blue.

https://youtu.be/wTQu0dZ8DEQ

35 –

All the blue and light colliding
With the silver skyscrapers and
Those two Towers
Twin Towers
Stretching like arms robotic arms
Stretching up and into
Into the blue trapezoid sky.

https://youtu.be/ds22OShghcc

36 –

From the ground the sky was a
Trapezoid
A trapezoid caught in-between
The Twin Towers rising up
Into the blue geometric sky.

https://youtu.be/mwTNrY04zhU

37 –

The Twin Towers were there
Luminous and looming above
Creating a trapezoid sky. This
Sky and these two silver shining
Towers.

https://youtu.be/eHWtpe-2pxE

38 –

That is exactly how they were.
That is exactly how it was.
I know.
I know because I was there.

https://youtu.be/Tr31x2UcDmQ

39 –

I was on my way.
I was heading downtown
Until we stopped.
The subway stopped and I got off.
I got off the subway and emerged
Out from below, out into this day
With the Twin Towers stretching up
Making a trapezoid blue sky above me.

https://youtu.be/-LLU6MTiV38

40 –

I did not stop, not yet.
I was still walking.
I was still walking until
Something made me stop
And look up.

https://youtu.be/eO-6Roaxd-E

41 –

There I was
On that day in this moment
Standing there, on the corner
Of Worth and Church,
Looking up.
Looking up into the blue trapezoid sky.
Looking up at those two Twin Towers
Spinning in the sky like that,
Like robotic arms, silver and metallic and shining,
Like they were, and like I cannot explain.

https://youtu.be/J6s6AYQOLIs

42 –

And I remember this.
I can tell you this.
I was thinking
About how lucky I was,
At that moment, that exact moment.

https://youtu.be/bchptvdreRA

43 –

I was going to be a lawyer,
This life of rules and codes
Where everything has a place.
That is what I thought.
I was walking from the subway
And I felt like I was missing it,
Missing this city, and missing
My time, my time in it.
At that moment, I stopped
And I looked up and I saw
That sky and I was transfixed.

https://youtu.be/271xoRb68ro

44 –

I was transfixed, fixed
To that corner, standing
There, looking up into
The blue trapezoid sky
With the two Twin Towers
Spinning and shining silver.
And I was feeling lucky.
I was thankful to it all,
To the sky, the Towers,
To this New York City
That was now mine.

https://youtu.be/4G2KwQAZSmc

45 –

But life is not law.
Life and what happens in it
Is not patriotic to rules or codes,
And that is why.
In an irony as deeply set as lungs
Within a rib cage, it happened,
The breath of the next moment.
Because as I was looking up
At that sky, decoding it as a sign,
My sign, at the Twin Towers so silver,
It happened.

https://youtu.be/85qs10etEyg

46 –

But it happened slowly
As if in a set of movie stills,
Or slow motion, part by part
Until it was over.

https://youtu.be/T9GGb_qikxQ

47 –

As I stood there, on that corner,
The corner of Church and Worth
Looking up into the perfect blue sky,
Looking at the Twin Towers like arms,
Shining and silver arms reaching up
Rotating and retracting and spinning
In this, the trapezoid sky, a plane.
A plane entered my plane of vision.

https://youtu.be/Fa6Z0Pgk0rc

48 –

I saw the plane and it was beautiful,
Beautiful before I knew,
Beautiful like a smooth white bird
Gliding towards the Twin Towers.
Later they would say how
It severed a stairway.
It severed a stairway
Like a head from a body.
And how the people below,
They tried to get out.
And how the people above,
They were trapped.

https://youtu.be/xO0S0UIxaK4

49 –

But at that moment I was not thinking
About the people on the plane or about
The people in the North Tower.
I was seeing. I was only seeing,
Seeing this, an image unfolding.
As I stood there, standing there
On the corner of Church and Worth
And watched.

https://youtu.be/8fTsnHQ37WA

50 –

How can I describe
The way it happened
How can I describe
The way it looked
What words can I use?

https://youtu.be/kNLZqwzJKSg

51 –

All I can tell you about is the image,
The image they played again and
Again on the news, over and over,
And about how it looked to me,
In that moment, the moment
That it happened,
While I stood there,
And watched.

https://youtu.be/H7rSRaY8FIk

52 –

The plane crashed into the North Tower,
A silent crash, a burst in my memory.
It left a hole, with shiny silver metal
Shooting out around it.
It was a jagged hole
With twisted silver metal
And a black center.
This black hole, it was an iris popping out.
From down below I imagined it was hot.
Serene and still and silent,
A black hole suspended there
Against a blue trapezoid sky.

https://youtu.be/roEbgAzUXcQ

53 –

And then I went to class.
While the smoke started to cover,
Cover the sky, cover the blue sky.
While the news started to cover,
Cover the accident, cover this,
What we thought was
An accident of a plane crashing
Into a Tower.

https://youtu.be/dmkM6Nm9a2E

54 –

This was before, the time before,
Before anyone knew, really knew,
What it really was.
This was the time in-between, before
Before everyone realized it was more,
More than this, more than a plane hitting
A Tower, more than people dying, more.

https://youtu.be/9QRCeSHSjXM

55 –

But before I knew, before anyone
Knew what it was, I called my mother and I said,
There's been an accident and *turn on the news*,
And *because*, I said, *because it just happened.*

https://youtu.be/LCEYNaf1Q98

56 –

Later, much later, later that day, and one day
Later and two days later, I watched the news.
I would sit in my apartment
And I would watch the news.
I would watch the news and how they covered 9/11,
Covered the plane crashing into the Tower,
Covered what I had seen, playing it again and again.

https://youtu.be/GyDEAwj0RbY

57 –

The news coverage playing it on a constant loop
Of a plane crash hole and a plane crash hole.
Playing it like that over and over,
So that what really happened to me
Was almost lost.

https://youtu.be/d0P_Hn2EHgw

58 –

The news covering it all up,
Until almost nothing remained of me
And my memory and what happened
To me that day,
Except this, the news coverage, played
Over and over.
But that was after, that was after.

https://youtu.be/PyXj6wOTaqY

59 –

Now I was going inside.
I went inside and I went
Up to class.
And the professor was lecturing,
Talking about liability and claims
And the intent to do harm.
And outside there was a Tower
With a hole in it and people inside.

https://youtu.be/qZ__oxY6OXo

60 –

People's cell phones were ringing
And people were pacing the room,
Talking on their phones, apologizing
To the class, saying *I know someone.*
Because some of us knew someone
Someone who was in the North Tower.
And even if we didn't, didn't know someone
We all knew that there were people there,
Trapped in the North Tower.

https://youtu.be/VdU6r0r1odA

61 –

Then we heard it, and we ran
Over to the window and saw it.
We saw more smoke coming,
This time from the South Tower
And we knew.
We knew there was another one,
Another plane and another crash.

https://youtu.be/w0voQUoGjcY

62 –

We knew another Tower had been hit,
Another Tower filled with more people.
We knew that there was another hole now,
Black and jagged and hot, and how
How all those people were trapped.
And we knew.
We knew that this was not an accident.
We knew that this was something else.

https://youtu.be/D9g0xY1wYCg

63 –

But this was law school, and we were
In class and the professor was talking.
He was still talking to us about law,
About liability and claims and intent.
And we kept taking notes, because
He did not stop, and we did not stop
Because we knew that if we stopped,
We would fail.
And as he was talking about the law,
People were crying and screaming.

https://youtu.be/uJx5SXgqwGM

64 –

Cell phones were ringing and people
Were crying and screaming and running
Over to the window to see.
But the professor was still talking
And he did not stop,
Even though we knew
People were dying.
And he did not stop talking until,
Until someone came and told us
Get out.

https://youtu.be/dl30ZVYme9Q

65 –

And that is when
We left.
Someone told us to take the stairs,
Because the elevator was not working
Or because the elevator might stop,
Or because maybe it might blow up.

https://youtu.be/57zQlQvf5UQ

66 –

And it was quiet.
I remember thinking
About how quiet we were, all of us,
Evacuating down, down those stairs.
We were like cows or horses, a herd.
Corralled by circumstance. We were
Stuck together in this stairway, stuck
In this day, stuck in this disaster, just
Stuck. We were stuck in this together.

https://youtu.be/5V-5wyEU3As

67 –

Years before, when I was just a girl,
I went to the Statue of Liberty, and
I climbed up to her crown, up and up.
And how the stairway was small and
Spiraling, so narrow, how
There was nowhere to go, and I was
Stuck there.
And in this stairway, on 9/11,
I was thinking *I will never do that again.*
Not after this, not ever again.
If there was an ever again.
As I evacuated down that stairway on 9/11,
I was thinking, wondering
If I would even live.

https://youtu.be/K8i44cYgLCs

68 –

Because in that moment I knew.
I knew that *this might be it,* that
I might, I might die down there,
Down out there,
On the street where the world
Was splitting and cracking in half.

https://youtu.be/v_uLYANFjtI

69 –

People were in those Towers
And planes had hit them,
Those Towers
And those people in them,
Hit, hit, and gone
And now two holes.

https://youtu.be/jWAunmS0wPU

70 –

New York City is an island
And on an island like this,
There is nowhere,
There is nowhere to go
Once you get to the end.
I knew that.
Even then,
When I was on those stairs,
I knew that,
That this could be the end.
Just like when I was a girl
Climbing the Statue of Liberty,
I could not turn around.
I could only go in this direction.
I could only go down.

https://youtu.be/gpiDrSdg9ps

71 –

All of us together, a chain
Of us, law students on stairs,
Going down into a world
Where rules were gone.
And when we got down,
Got down to the first floor
And into the lobby,
A man stood there.
He was an administrator,
This man I did not know.
And he told us we had a choice.
He told us we could stay,
Go under the ground,
Under the school in a bomb shelter,
Or we could run.

https://youtu.be/wI-ik1tIyYY

72 –

They told us we could stay,
Go underground into a bomb
Shelter, or that we could run.
And I remember,
How I did not know what to do.

https://youtu.be/liBpFt9_dng

73 –

I remember waiting in line
There in the lobby, waiting
For a telephone, for my turn.
We were all waiting there,
In a long line like a snake.
Waiting for those telephones
Because all of our cell phones
Were dead now.

https://youtu.be/ssTWUvTHKfI

74 –

And the telephone was warm
When it was my turn, and when
I held it up to my cheek, warm
From the girl before me, warm
Because she was still alive.

https://youtu.be/FZBbZle5IxE

75 –

I called my mother again, a wire
Stretching across highways and over
A river, and up the side of the house
That I grew up in, then into a receiver
Cradling my mother's cheek, cradling.
I was cradling my mother's cheek.

https://youtu.be/38bJSj_t6Zg

76 –

On the telephone when it was my turn
I told my mother what had happened and how,
I told her that I had a choice, how I could stay
Here in the school, underground or I could go
And run for my life.
And I asked her, I asked my mother
What should I do?
And she said *I cannot tell you,*
How she could not tell me,
She could not tell me what to do.
Just like that and my turn was over
And my mother, her voice, was gone.

https://youtu.be/E39u-BKwKGU

77 –

I did not know what to do.
I did not know if I should stay,
Go underground into the bomb shelter
Or if I should start running.

https://youtu.be/4PG5XY6XaAc

78 –

I remember how I went out.
I went outside, just to think,
And to be outside, in the air,
So I can breathe, I thought.
And when I got outside
I stood on that same corner,
The corner of Church and of Worth,
And I stood there.
I stood there, just thinking
And watching, watching
All of the smoke and fire
Like a flag coming out,
Coming out from the holes.
The holes from the planes
On those two Towers.

https://youtu.be/H8qo7sqHGic

79 –

Other people were on the corner
Standing and watching too and
They were crying and screaming.
They were crying and screaming
Because the world was cracking
In half, splitting apart, breaking.

https://youtu.be/qx_uy73MDuA

80 –

The world was cracking, splitting, breaking
As I stood there on that corner watching.
And then it happened.
People started jumping.

https://youtu.be/ykDiy8lLBvw

81 –

People were jumping out
Of the North Tower.
They were, the people were jumping
Out of the windows. People from the
North Tower were falling from the sky.

https://youtu.be/QlUmuNtGLrI

82 –

They were the people who worked there,
Who were trapped there, trapped in that
Tower, a Tower on fire, in the blue sky.
And now they were jumping.
They were jumping out of the North Tower
And they were all falling.
They were falling from the sky.

https://youtu.be/ch-9Yr_YBZ8

83 –

From where I stood, on that corner,
The people falling down were small,
Small like dolls.
I saw the people climbing out,
Out of the windows, holding on
And sliding down.
I saw the people sliding down
The sides of the North Tower,
Trying to hang on, like they
Were just trying to hang on,
Before, before they had to let go,
Let it all go.

https://youtu.be/s0SbgWY0jvQ

84 –

I saw the people, standing in open windows
And then, jumping, jumping out, and falling,
Falling through the air.
I saw the people falling through the air,
Slipping past the blue sky, their clothing
Ballooning around them like parachutes.

https://youtu.be/h2exB0S1hHw

85 –

They're jumping I yelled.
They're jumping I whispered.
And all I could do was this,
Stand and watch.
And all I could think was how,
How their bodies looked small like dolls,
How they did not look real, falling like that,
With their blouses and pants and suit jackets
And skirts ballooning around them like parachutes
As they somersaulted and cartwheeled in the sky.

https://youtu.be/XA_7pj-YNkI

86 –

They were people.
People somersaulting and cartwheeling
Down in the sky.
They were businessmen and businesswomen,
Mothers and fathers, sisters
And brothers, sons, daughters,
Friends, rivals, lovers, strangers,
All of them, all of them, people.

https://youtu.be/BB-n_jiExjo

87 –

And now they were falling, tumbling
Through the sky like tiny gymnasts.
Knees brought up to chests, arms
Raising up to the sky, legs extended
Out, flying, flying like gymnasts.
I remember how some,
Some of them jumped
Out of the Tower in pairs.
I remember seeing them
Fall through that sky
In tandem, falling away
From one another, and
Then, falling back into
One another.

https://youtu.be/VSeFq6yBmWE

88 –

And I remember how
When they fell out of my line of vision,
How there were more, more people,
More bodies, always more.

https://youtu.be/NzEzutnNqik

89 –

They were people.
People jumping out of the North Tower,
People falling down from the sky.
And they were going to land,
Land somewhere.

https://youtu.be/N5TrQTeGirs

90 –

They were going to land
On the ground, this same
Ground I was standing on,
The ground 13 blocks away.
That ground 13 blocks away,
That ground that would give way,
That would sink into itself, a ready
Grave, this ground, this ground
That would become Ground Zero.

https://youtu.be/wXxhxM7pL2E

91 –

That ground, a hole,
Another hole.
Years later, I would read how
It was only 12 seconds. How
It only took 12 seconds
For the people falling,
The people jumping
To hit the ground.
And how
Someone had stood there
In Battery Park, counting.

https://youtu.be/pEwlHsuW7ko

92 –

What I know is this.
This is where I was
During those 12 seconds,
The last 12 seconds of their lives,
The people who jumped, who fell,
Their lives, I was there.
I was standing there, on the corner
Of Church and Worth, that corner
Where my belief lost meaning.
I was standing there
Watching.

https://youtu.be/BT4ldHD9HLA

93 –

But it was only minutes,
Just minutes, this collection of
12 seconds, a collection of people
In flight, a collection of their bodies
Collecting on the ground
Just 13 blocks away.
I watched them fall from the sky
For only a few minutes.

https://youtu.be/4tueFPqyi_k

94 –

Because now,
Now the Tower was collapsing.
The South Tower was collapsing,
Collapsing.
The South Tower was collapsing,
Collapsing down.

https://youtu.be/Ok1HuoD-cCw

95 –

It's collapsing I whispered.
Collapsing.
Collapsing down I said, louder now.
And I did not think.
I did not think about it,
The geometry of a fall
Or the force of gravity.
I did not think about
The impact of a Tower
Falling, flying, going
Down.

https://youtu.be/QGlHLcN1yF0

96 –

I just watched it.
I watched it buckle.
I watched it shake.
I watched it fall,
Fall inward, the Tower
Falling into itself, a motion
Of implosion, silent explosion
Turned inside out.
And how it looked.
How it looked when it crumbled,
The metal and asbestos and glass,
That Tower, those bodies, all of it,
Crumbling.

https://youtu.be/ksvLDfBRjdw

97 –

This is how,
How the South Tower fell.
First there was a rumble,
Soft noise, how it was a soft noise.
Soft like thunder or traffic,
Somewhere else in a place
Called distance, *like it isn't*,
I said, *like it isn't real.*
And then it got louder.
It started to roar, roar
As it fell, because it was,
It was real.
It was really happening.

https://youtu.be/5miUEVYwlZY

98 –

It collapsed and crashed down.
And people, people standing
Here, on the corner with me,
Were collapsing in the street,
Crashing down, crying out *no*.
Because it was crashing, almost
Disintegrating, disintegrating as,
As it fell, into a dust, a thick dust.
It is a dust made up of the Tower
And the bodies and my memories.

https://youtu.be/tno9wBxn8pA

99 –

And it poured down, covering everything.
Covering the streets and the people and
Everything below it.
Because when a Tower falls,
It has to go somewhere and
Become something, something else.

https://youtu.be/GEWRMv7jQTA

100 –

And the dust was moving towards me,
A toxic tornado whipping towards me,
Towards where I was standing,
Standing there, on that corner
13 blocks away.
And I know now.
I know how dust is.
How dust can erase everything in its wake,
Leaving behind this,
A dust city with dust bodies
Lying like clay on the ground.
I know now, how
Dust can bury you.
How dust can bury you alive.

https://youtu.be/TxK7hkIK-Es

101 –

But then, then I just stood there
Watching, watching the Tower fall.
Buckling and shaking and falling
And crumbling, crumbling down.
And that is when,
When I decided.
I decided,
I decided to run.

https://youtu.be/eo79u58D5L8

102 –

And I was running.
I was running with the South Tower
Collapsing behind me.
And I was running.
Running for my life.

https://youtu.be/H6uG1pH0hqQ

103 –

I remember the dust.
How when the South Tower
Crashed down, there was this
Dust. There was falling metal
And bodies and dust.
An explosion of dust.
And the dust was moving,
Moving quickly, covering
The streets and the people
On them, covering them
And I was running.
I was running away,
Away from the falling Tower,
Away from it,
Away from the dust.

https://youtu.be/kGhtTQ9AybE

104 –

Later I would think about it.
About the dust, about how
It had the power to erase,
Erase everything in its path,
Even me.

https://youtu.be/xAndnaA4fgk

105 –

And as I ran, thought,
Thought about it, about
How, how I might die.
And I thought about the others.
I thought about the people
Trapped in those Towers.
I thought about the people
Who jumped out.

https://youtu.be/_cEx2eDnbLM

106 –

I thought about the people
In my class, how some of them
Went underground and some,
Some ran the other way, down
To the tip of this island, where
The land meets the water and
Where there was nowhere
Left to go. All of us, all of us,
And the dust,
With nowhere left to go, with
Nowhere, nowhere left to go.

https://youtu.be/gEfk2xFOJO4

107 –

And how,
How it made the city look,
The dust, how it made it look
Like a fossil, like the world broke,
Broke in half, and this was it, all
That was left, the outline of bones
And buildings underneath the dust.

https://youtu.be/cCHqnc0VhT4

108 –

I remember saying *no*,
Putting my hands up, up in front of me,
As if I could block the dust, as if I could
Block the sky.
And how I heard it, my voice.
I heard my voice saying it,
Saying *no*.
And how, how I ran through it,
Through my voice saying *no*,
These particles dissolving already.

https://youtu.be/ckGxVXBuVYU

109 –

There were no cars driving
On the streets
But I saw cars. I saw cars,
Parked and pulled over,
Off on the side of the street.
Some cars were abandoned,
More metal scrapped, doors
Open, just these metal shells.
There were people sitting on top
Of the roofs of other cars, sitting
There and looking back at them,
The Twin Towers, a space, that
Space in the sky.

https://youtu.be/97Hs7ARSrKo

110 –

That space in the sky, a space
Forming where the South Tower
Used to be. And car radios were
Blasting the news.
And the news anchors were saying
Things like how, how *a Twin Tower*
Just fell.

https://youtu.be/tklKTOvX5JA

111 –

And how people kicked off
Their shoes,
How they left them there,
These heaps of it, of shoes
And briefcases.
But I kept carrying my books.
I did not leave my books.
I could not leave them there
Because if I did, it would mean
That this, this was happening,
That this was really happening.

https://youtu.be/u7Sgqi5vP0Y

112 –

Because it did,
It did happen.
And suddenly there was
This sound. There was a
Sound, the sound of metal
And it was cracking.
The North Tower cracking
In half.

https://youtu.be/GBgUfJ51QBU

113 –

And then there was a boom.
The kind of boom
That thunder cannot make.
The kind of noise I have never heard,
Never before, a kind of noise I do not
Think I will ever hear, hear again.
The kind of boom buildings make,
When they fall.
This was the noise the North Tower
Made when it fell, fell
Down, down to the ground.

https://youtu.be/ImNYtGC9vYw

114 –

And I was looking, looking
Over my shoulder
And I could see it,
The new smoke, all of it,
I could see more dust.
And I knew.
I already knew.
I knew that it was the other Tower.
I knew that the North Tower was falling.

https://youtu.be/RoayKI2vp-U

115 –

The North Tower was falling too.
So I ran faster.
I ran faster and I ran away,
Away from metal cracking,
Away from the Towers falling
And away from dust forming,
Forming a giant sea behind me.

https://youtu.be/LKiu9Nm6PYU

116 –

And I kept running until I couldn't,
Couldn't run anymore, until I fell,
Fell down in the street, and until
He picked me up, a man I didn't know.
He picked me up, his hands and fingers
Under my armpits, heaved me up into
A standing position, asking me, *what*,
And *what is your name*, telling me,
Telling me how I was *fine*,
How I was *still fine*.

https://youtu.be/ZbcJWYP9RuU

117 –

And I do not remember,
Remember if I said it out loud
To the man who helped me in the street,
How I wanted to,
Wanted to tell them,
My parents, tell them *I am still alive.*

https://youtu.be/8BNxLGH_OmI

118 –

And he was pointing, this man,
Up to a building, to the second
Floor of a building, there, across
The street.
He was saying how, how it was an
Advertising company, how he knew
Someone, someone who worked there,
How it was empty,
But how,
How it had a telephone I could use.

https://youtu.be/CGTTqjdrJiY

119 –

And I followed him,
This man I did not know,
A man who picked me up,
Picked me up by my armpits
After I fell down in the street.
I followed him across the street
And up a fire escape, a metal
Ladder, up the side of a building
Through a window, into an office,
Where I called, called my mother,
Called her and told her *I am still alive*.

https://youtu.be/m75ILcQnpRM

120 –

And then I was back on a street,
Walking now, walking all the way
Uptown,
All those blocks up,
All the way uptown.

https://youtu.be/MsauTZbMsx0

121 –

In some way 9/11 is that.
A series of connections and
Disconnections, of telephone
Calls, the ones that went through
And the ones, the ones that did not.

https://youtu.be/QO7CjAnYNr4

122 –

Later when I finally got there,
Back to my apartment on 79th Street,
When I turned my key in a lock and
Found my dog, waiting for me, found
Everything just as it was before,
I tried to call me parents again
But my telephone did not work.

https://youtu.be/YFtOVKOrms4

123 –

And I remember e-mailing people,
People I used to know, who lived,
Lived far away from this, asking
Them, *please*, to please call them,
Call my parents and tell them
I am alive.

https://youtu.be/xTbjjB7S2bs

124 –

Because that was the question
In the days that followed, as I
Walked around the city, seeing
Signs posted everywhere with
Pictures of smiling faces
Of the people lost,
Lost in the rubble,
Covered by metal and dust and
Other bodies, the question of
Whether or not they were still alive.
And the first responders dug,
Dug into the dust and rubble,
Each scoop of a shovel,
A possible answer.

https://youtu.be/WFIcZ5t05DM

125 –

And I saw the first responders
With their dogs, when I went back,
Two weeks later, back to school,
Past the security checkpoints,
And into the dust surrounding
Ground Zero, and past the shoes,
Laying on the ground, forgotten.
Past the papers shuffling in the wind,
Past the rescue people with boots,
Boots caked with what was left there,
Left in that hole.

https://youtu.be/I_5QugFoIls

126 –

I wore a mask
And I remember thinking, thinking
How, how I could feel it in my lungs,
The dust, and what it was, how this
Was a burial ground.
I went back to school for a few days
Until I could not do it anymore, not
With the dust and digging
Of Ground Zero below me.
And so I left,
I left law school
And I left New York City.

https://youtu.be/_3TuhVMng-M

127 –

Almost ten years after
I went back to Ground Zero, back to the site,
Where the planes hit and the bodies jumped
And the Towers fell, while I just stood there,
On the street below, looking up, and watching.

https://youtu.be/oIezQwa9Bow

128 –

And I walked around Ground Zero, circling
Its high metal fences, policemen and barricades,
Meant to control the crowds, crowds of tourists
With their cameras clicking and I am here again,
Back on the corner, the same corner I stood on,
All those years ago, watching it happen.

https://youtu.be/yJAgLeXenIw

129 –

And I was looking down the same street,
At the same space, the space where there
Used to be Towers, and then emptiness
And now cranes and scaffolding and I am
Looking up at the same building I was in
When the second plane hit.
And I am thinking about it,
About the tourists with their cameras,
And me, me with my memories, all of us,
Holding onto it,
Holding onto 9/11,
Holding onto it, as if,
As if disaster is something you can keep.

https://youtu.be/XMxOeBFfohk

130 –

And it is like the sky,
Like the sky that day,
On 9/11,
Just before it happened,
That imprint of blue and silver,
Gone now,
But there, always there.

https://youtu.be/qNeW0r7fH5M

Coda

How do you acknowledge
All who were lost
That day, who fell from the sky or jumped,
Crushed on impact, crashing down, or after,
Who ran inside and did not, did not come out,
Or even, even after that,
Who got sick, toxic lungs, fast-splitting cells,
Those who survived but then
Could not –

Except to say, *I dream of you*
And *always*.

A memory is what happens,
Wing of a plane slicing through cloud
A torso of a woman found in rubble,
Fingers clutching metal, or
How *we hang on.*

Because preservation is something,
Something we do. So that, so that
We never forget.

A Few Words of Thanks

Thank you to Stephen Farrell for publishing my poems, "Adjustments," "Drones," "Know," and "Where" in *The New York Times* in 2010 and 2011, and for publishing my poetic essay "From A Military Wife, Words on War" in 2011 at the stunningly important "At War" blog at *The New York Times*. It is through Farrell that my poems about war were first shared with readers on a global scale.

Thank you to James Dao for publishing my essay "Search Engines Log the Fearsome Journeys of War Families" at *The New York Times* in 2012.

Thank you to my agent Heather Mitchell of the Gelfman Schneider Literary Agency, for taking me on in 2010, for representing me for more than a decade, and for believing in my poetry.

Thank you to my co-editors at *The Wrath Bearing Tree* for always supporting my poetry—and all poetry—and for championing social justice through writing.

Thank you to these fellow war-writers for their kind words and insights in reviewing *September Eleventh* prior to publication: Pamela Hart, author of *Mothers Over Nangarhar* and writer-in-residence at the Katonah Museum of Art; Adrian Bonenberger, author of *The Disappointed Soldier and Other Stories from War* and a founding co-editor of *The Wrath-Bearing Tree*; and Lisa Stice, author of *Forces, Permanent Change of Station*, and *Uniform*.

Thank you to every single person who has read my poems, thought about them, and shared them. It is my one true belief that we are all connected, especially so through our stories.

And to those who were lost on September 11, 2011, and after, in the aftermath, I carry you, deeply, always, in my heart.

About the Author

Amalie Flynn is a poet and the author of *Wife and War: The Memoir* (2013) and a collection of poetry blogs: *September Eleventh, Wife and War, The Sustainability of Us*, and *Border of Heartbreak*. Flynn's writing has appeared in *The New York Times*, *Time* magazine, and *The Huffington Post*, and has received mentions from *The New York Times* and CNN.

Flynn has an undergraduate degree in English / Studio Arts from Trinity College, Hartford, Connecticut; a Master of Fine Arts degree in creative writing from the University of Alabama, Tuscaloosa; and a doctorate in humanities from Salve Regina University, Newport, Rhode Island. She serves as poetry editor for the on-line literary journal *The Wrath-Bearing Tree*. Flynn lives in Rhode Island with her husband and their two children.

You can learn more about her on-line at:
https://septembereleventh.wordpress.com/

Follow her on Facebook: www.facebook.com/Amalie-Flynn-Author-221024301241286/

Follow her on Twitter: @amalieflynn

Did You Enjoy This Book?

Tell your friends and family about it, or post your thoughts via social media sites, like Facebook and Twitter! On-line communities that serve military families, veterans, and service members are also ideal places to help spread the word about this book, and others like it!

You can also share a quick review on websites for other readers, such as Goodreads.com. Or offer a few of your impressions on bookseller websites, such as Amazon.com and BarnesandNoble.com!

Better yet, recommend the title to your favorite local librarian, poetry society or book club leader, museum gift store manager, or independent bookseller! There is nothing more powerful in business of publishing than a shared review or recommendation from a friend.

We appreciate your support! We'll continue to look for new stories and voices to share with our readers. Keep in touch!

You can write us at:

Middle West Press LLC
P.O. Box 1153
Johnston, Iowa 50131-9420

Or visit: www.middlewestpress.com

❖   ❖   ❖

Other poetry collections from Middle West Press LLC:

Permanent Change of Station
and *Forces*
by Lisa Stice

Hugging This Rock:
Poems of Earth & Sky, Love & War
by Eric Chandler

135

How to Access the Micro-Videos

On each page, readers of the e-book edition of this book will also find a YouTube link to a companion micro-video read by the author.

Rather than input links manually, readers of the print edition can access all the videos by scanning the QR code below:

❖　❖　❖

https://www.youtube.com/channel/
UCKNqU0BTVFLUNC6fA72pEXw/videos